# Mini
## Early Elementary

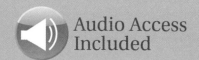
Audio Access Included

# A DOZEN A DAY
# CHRISTMAS

T0070495

Orchestrated Accompaniments by Eric Baumgartner

The price of this publication includes access to audio tracks online for download or streaming, using the unique code below.

To access audio visit:
**www.halleonard.com/mylibrary**

Enter Code
6956-0162-2789-3750

ISBN 978-1-4950-2688-1

EXCLUSIVELY DISTRIBUTED BY

WILLIS MUSIC

HAL•LEONARD®
CORPORATION
7777 W. BLUEMOUND RD. P.O. BOX 13819
MILWAUKEE, WISCONSIN 53213

# NOTE TO TEACHERS

This collection of Christmas favorites can be used on its own or as supplementary material to the iconic *A Dozen A Day* technique series by Edna Mae Burnam. The pieces have been arranged to progress gradually, applying concepts and patterns from Burnam's technical exercises whenever possible. Optional accompaniments are also provided for teachers or older students.

These arrangements are excellent supplements for any method and may also be used for sight-reading practice for more advanced students.

# Jolly Old St. Nicholas

Traditional 19th Century American Carol
*Arranged by Carolyn Miller*

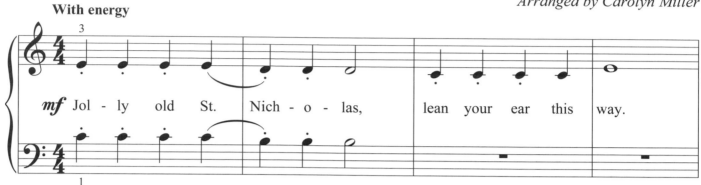

Jol - ly old St. Nich - o - las, lean your ear this way.

Don't you tell a sin - gle soul what I'm going to say.

**Accompaniment** (Student plays one octave higher than written.)

Christ - mas Eve is com - ing soon. Now, you dear old man,

whis - per what you'll bring to me; tell me if you

can.

# O Come, O Come, Emmanuel

Traditional Latin Text
15th Century French Melody
Adapted by Thomas Helmore
*Arranged by Carolyn Miller*

**Accompaniment** (Student plays one octave higher than written.)

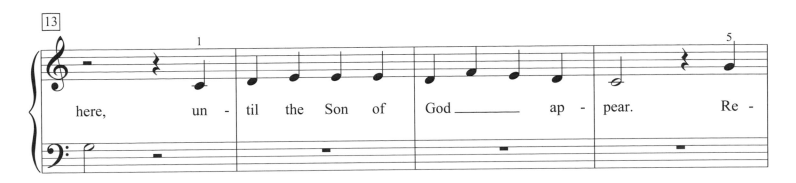

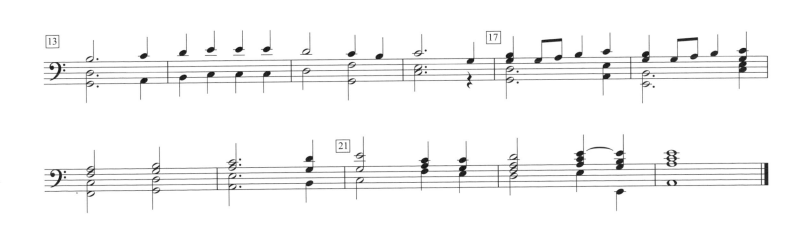

# Good King Wenceslas

Words by John M. Neale<br>
Music from Piae Cantiones<br>
Arranged by Carolyn Miller

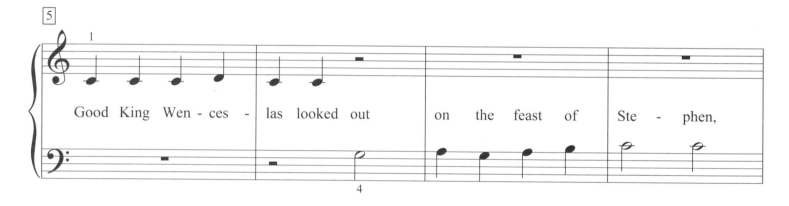

Good King Wen - ces - las looked out　on the feast of　Ste - phen,

**Accompaniment** (Student plays one octave higher than written.)

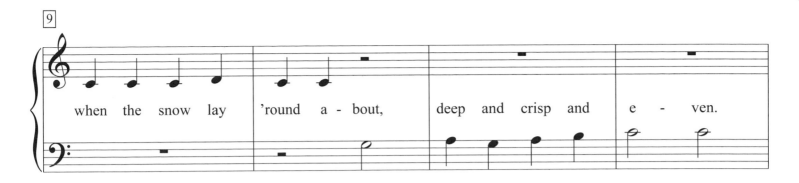

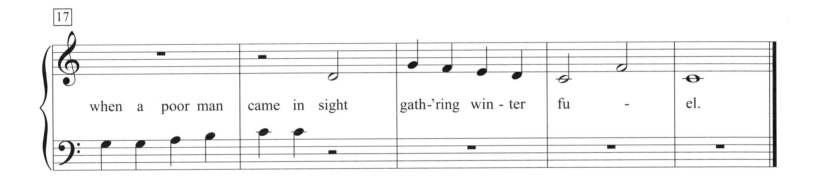

# O Come, All Ye Faithful

Music by John Francis Wade
Latin Words translated by Frederick Oakeley
*Arranged by Carolyn Miller*

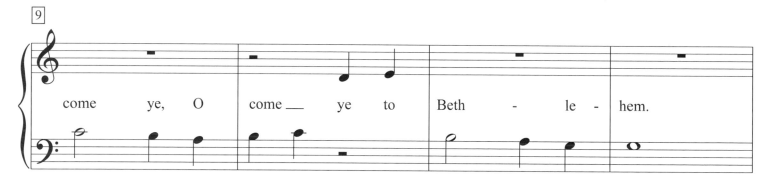

**Accompaniment** (Student plays one octave higher than written.)

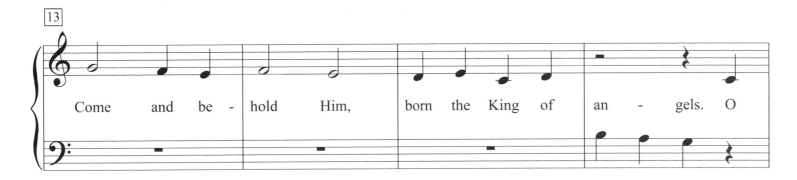

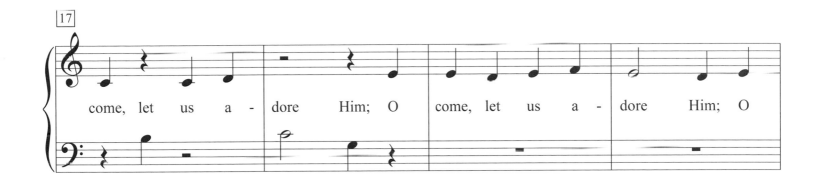

# Bring a Torch, Jeannette, Isabella

17th Century French Provençal Carol
*Arranged by Carolyn Miller*

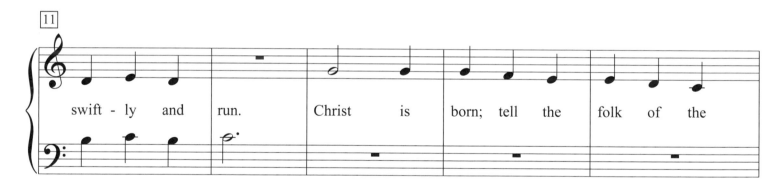

**Accompaniment** (Student plays one octave higher than written.)

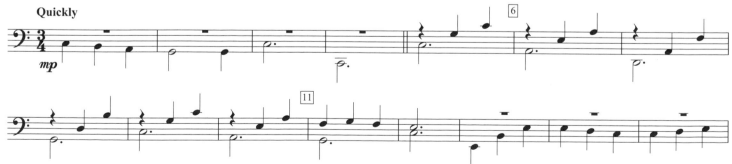

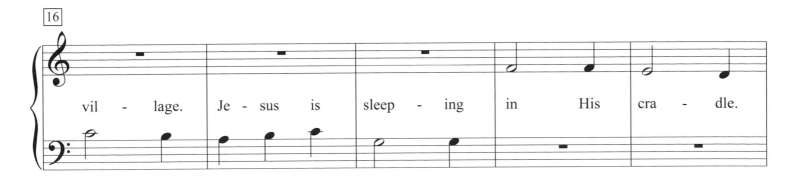

# O Little Town of Bethlehem

Words by Phillips Brooks
Music by Lewis H. Redner
*Arranged by Carolyn Miller*

**Accompaniment** (Student plays one octave higher than written.)

# Away in a Manger

Traditional Words
Music by James R. Murray
*Arranged by Carolyn Miller*

**Accompaniment** (Student plays one octave higher than written.)

# Still, Still, Still

Salzburg Melody, c. 1819
Traditional Austrian Text
*Arranged by Carolyn Miller*

Still, __ still, __ still; while __ we Thy vig - il __ keep. And __

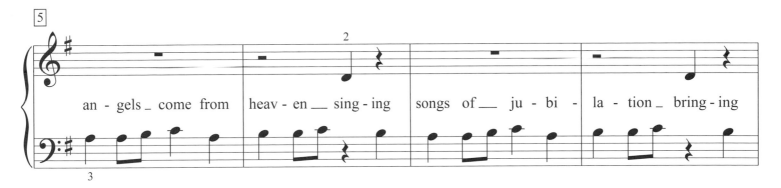

an - gels __ come from heav - en __ sing - ing songs of __ ju - bi - la - tion __ bring - ing

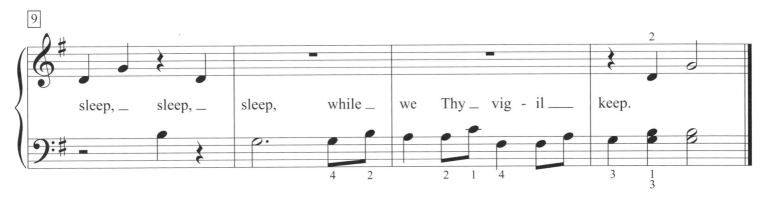

sleep, __ sleep, __ sleep, while __ we Thy __ vig - il __ keep.

**Accompaniment** (Student plays one octave higher than written.)

# Up on the Housetop

Words and Music by
B.R. Hanby
*Arranged by Carolyn Miller*

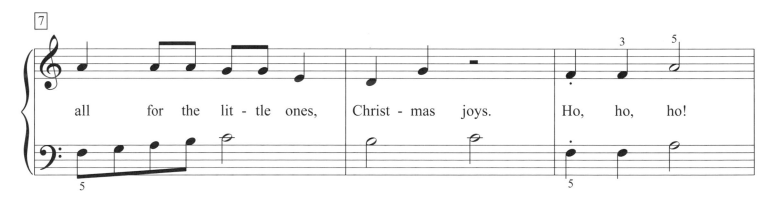

**Accompaniment** (Student plays one octave higher than written.)

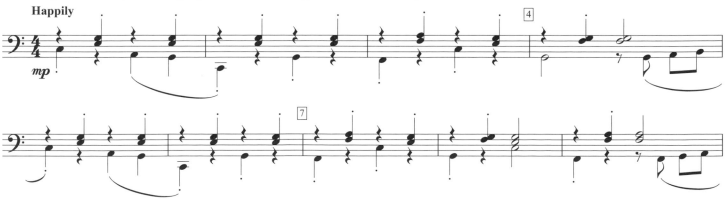

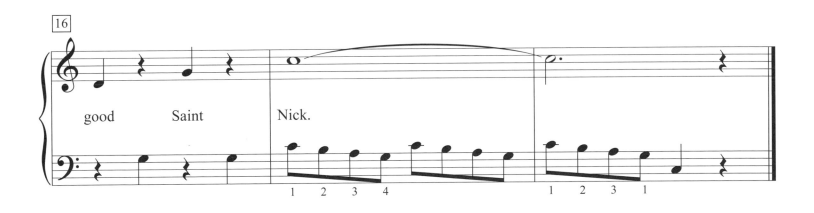

# What Child Is This?

Words by William C. Dix
16th Century English Melody
*Arranged by Carolyn Miller*

**Accompaniment** (Student plays one octave higher than written.)

# A DOZEN A DAY

## by Edna Mae Burnam

The **A Dozen A Day** books are universally recognized as one of the most remarkable technique series on the market for all ages! Each book in this series contains short warm-up exercises to be played at the beginning of each practice session, providing excellent day-to-day training for the student. The CD is playable on any CD player and features fabulous backing tracks by Ric Iannone. For Windows® and Mac users, the CD is enhanced so you can access MIDI files for each exercise and adjust the tempo.

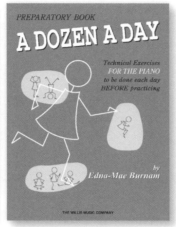

**MINI BOOK**
00404073  Book Only ..................... $4.99
00406472  Book/CD ..................... $9.99

**PREPARATORY BOOK**
00414222  Book Only ..................... $4.99
00406476  Book/CD ..................... $9.99

**BOOK 1**
00413366  Book Only ..................... $4.99
00406481  Book/CD ..................... $9.99

**BOOK 2**
00413826  Book Only ..................... $4.99
00406485  Book/CD ..................... $9.99

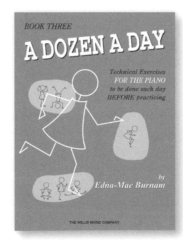
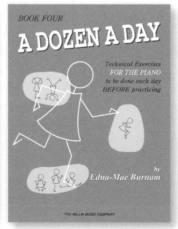

**BOOK 3**
00414136  Book Only ..................... $5.99
00416760  Book/CD ..................... $10.99

**BOOK 4**
00415686  Book Only ..................... $5.99
00416761  Book/CD ..................... $10.99

**PLAY WITH EASE IN MANY KEYS**
00416395  Book Only ..................... $4.99

**ALSO AVAILABLE:**

The **A Dozen A Day Songbook** series containing Broadway, movie, and pop hits!

Visit Hal Leonard Online at **www.halleonard.com**

EXCLUSIVELY DISTRIBUTED BY

Prices, contents, and availability subject to change without notice. Prices listed in U.S. funds.

0613

# A DOZEN A DAY SONGBOOK SERIES
## BROADWAY, MOVIE AND POP HITS
### Arranged by Carolyn Miller

The *A Dozen a Day Songbook* series contains wonderful Broadway, movie and pop hits that may be used as companion pieces to the memorable technique exercises in the *A Dozen a Day* series. They are also suitable as supplements for ANY method!

## MINI
EARLY ELEMENTARY
Songs in the Mini Book:
Any Dream Will Do • Can You Feel the Love Tonight • A Dream Is a Wish Your Heart Makes • Heigh-Ho • I'm Popeye the Sailor Man • It's a Grand Night for Singing • Lean on Me • Love Me Tender • So Long, Farewell • You'll Never Walk Alone.

00416858  Book Only ...................$6.99

00416861  Book/CD Pack..........$12.99

## PREPARATORY
MID-ELEMENTARY
Songs in the Preparatory Book:
The Bare Necessities • Do-Re-Mi • Getting to Know You • Heart and Soul • Little April Shower • Part of Your World • The Surrey with the Fringe on Top • Swinging on a Star • The Way You Look Tonight • Yellow Submarine.

00416859  Book Only ...................$6.99

00416862  Book/CD Pack..........$12.99

## BOOK 1
LATER ELEMENTARY
Songs in Book 1:
Cabaret • Climb Ev'ry Mountain • Give a Little Whistle • If I Were a Rich Man • Let It Be • Rock Around the Clock • Twist and Shout • The Wonderful Thing About Tiggers • Yo Ho (A Pirate's Life for Me) • Zip-A-Dee-Doo-Dah.

00416860  Book Only ..................$6.99

00416863  Book/CD Pack..........$12.99

## BOOK 2
EARLY INTERMEDIATE
Songs in Book 2:
Hallelujah • I Dreamed A Dream • I Walk the Line • I Want to Hold Your Hand • In the Mood • Moon River • Once Upon A Dream • This Land is Your Land • A Whole New World • You Raise Me Up.

00119241  Book Only ...................$6.99

00119242  Book/CD Pack ..........$12.99

Prices, content, and availability subject to change without notice.

WILLIS MUSIC

EXCLUSIVELY DISTRIBUTED BY

HAL•LEONARD®

**www.willispianomusic.com**       **www.facebook.com/willispianomusic**

0613

# TEACHING LITTLE FINGERS TO PLAY

## TEACHING LITTLE FINGERS TO PLAY

*by John Thompson*

A series for the early beginner combining rote and note approach. The melodies are written with careful thought and are kept as simple as possible, yet they are refreshingly delightful. All the music lies within the grasp of the child's small hands.

00412076  Book only .......................................$4.99
00406523  Book/CD ........................................$9.99

## TEACHING LITTLE FINGERS TO PLAY DISNEY TUNES

*arr. Glenda Austin*

10 delightful Disney songs with optional teacher accompaniments: The Bare Necessities • Can You Feel the Love Tonight • Candle on the Water • God Help the Outcasts • Kiss the Girl • Mickey Mouse March • The Siamese Cat Song • Winnie the Pooh • You'll Be in My Heart (Pop Version) • Zip-A-Dee-Doo-Dah.

00416748  Book only ......................................$6.99
00416749  Book/CD .......................................$12.99

## TEACHING LITTLE FINGERS TO PLAY CHRISTMAS CAROLS

*arr. Carolyn Miller*

12 piano solos with optional teacher accompaniments: Angels We Have Heard on High • Deck the Hall • The First Noel • Hark! The Herald Angels Sing • Jingle Bells • Jolly Old Saint Nicholas • Joy to the World! • O Come, All Ye Faithful • O Come Little Children • Silent Night • Up on the Housetop • We Three Kings of Orient Are.

00406391  Book ...........................................$5.99
00406722  Book/CD .......................................$10.99

## TEACHING LITTLE FINGERS TO PLAY CLASSICS

*arr. Randall Hartsell*

11 piano solo arrangements with optional teacher accompaniments: Bridal Chorus (from *Lohengrin*) (Wagner) • Can-Can (from *Orpheus in the Underworld*) (Offenbach) • Country Gardens (English Folk Tune) • A Little Night Music (from *Eine kleine Nachtmusik*) (Mozart) • Lullaby (Brahms) • Ode to Joy (from Symphony No. 9) (Beethoven) • Syphony No. 5 (Second Movement) (Tchaikovsky) • and more.

00406550  Book ...........................................$5.99
00406736  Book/CD .......................................$10.99

## TEACHING LITTLE FINGERS TO PLAY HYMNS

*arr. Mary K. Sallee*

11 hymns: Amazing Grace • Faith of Our Fathers • For the Beauty of the Earth • Holy, Holy, Holy • Jesus Loves Me • Jesus Loves the Little Children • Joyful, Joyful, We Adore Thee • Kum bah yah • Praise Him, All Ye Little Children • We Are Climbing Jacob's Ladder • What a Friend We Have in Jesus.

00406413  Book ...........................................$5.99
00406731  Book/CD .......................................$10.99

## TEACHING LITTLE FINGERS TO PLAY MORE

*by Leigh Kaplan*

*Teaching Little Fingers to Play More* is a fun-filled and colorfully illustrated follow-up book to *Teaching Little Fingers to Play*. This book strengthens skills learned while easing the transition into John Thompson's *Modern Course, Book One*.

00406137  Book only ......................................$5.99
00406527  Book/CD .......................................$9.99

## TEACHING LITTLE FINGERS TO PLAY MORE DISNEY TUNES

*arr. Glenda Austin*

9 songs, including: Circle of Life • Colors of the Wind • A Dream Is a Wish Your Heart Makes • A Spoonful of Sugar • Under the Sea • A Whole New World • and more.

00416750  Book only ......................................$6.99
00416751  Book/CD .......................................$12.99

## TEACHING LITTLE FINGERS TO PLAY MORE EASY DUETS

*arr. Carolyn Miller*

9 more fun duets arranged for 1 piano, 4 hands: A Bicycle Built for Two (Daisy Bell) • Blow the Man Down • Chopsticks • Do Your Ears Hang Low? • I've Been Working on the Railroad • The Man on the Flying Trapeze • Short'nin' Bread • Skip to My Lou • The Yellow Rose of Texas.

00416832  Book only ......................................$5.99
00416833  Book/CD .......................................$10.99

## TEACHING LITTLE FINGERS TO PLAY MORE BROADWAY SONGS

*arr. Carolyn Miller*

10 more fantastic Broadway favorites arranged for a young performer, including: Castle on a Cloud • Climb Ev'ry Mountain • Gary, Indiana • In My Own Little Corner • It's the Hard-Knock Life • Memory • Oh, What a Beautiful Mornin' • Sunrise, Sunset • Think of Me • Where Is Love?

00416928  Book only ......................................$6.99
00416929  Book/CD .......................................$12.99

## TEACHING LITTLE FINGERS TO PLAY MORE CHILDREN'S SONGS

*arr. by Carolyn Miller*

10 songs: The Candy Man • Do-Re-Mi • I'm Popeye the Sailor Man • It's a Small World • Linus and Lucy • The Muppet Show Theme • My Favorite Things • Sesame Street Theme • Supercalifragilisticexpialidocious • Tomorrow.

00416810  Book only ......................................$6.99
00416811  Book/CD .......................................$12.99

## TEACHING LITTLE FINGERS TO PLAY MORE CLASSICS

*arr. Randall Hartsell*

7 piano solos with optional teacher accompaniments: Marche Slave • Over the Waves • Polovtsian Dance (from the opera *Prince Igor*) • Pomp and Circumstance • Rondeau • Waltz (from the ballet *Sleeping Beauty*) • William Tell Overture.

00406760  Book only ......................................$5.99
00416513  Book/CD .......................................$10.99

**EXCLUSIVELY DISTRIBUTED BY**

**WILLIS MUSIC**

**HAL•LEONARD®**

7777 W. BLUEMOUND RD. P.O. BOX 13819
MILWAUKEE, WISCONSIN 53213

Prices, contents, and availability subject to change without notice.
Disney characters and artwork © Disney Enterprises, Inc.

**FOR A COMPLETE SERIES LISTING, VISIT WWW.HALLEONARD.COM**

0815